Day Tradin

MW01254876

A Powerful Intraday Strategy for Trading Stocks

Matthew R. Kratter

http://www.trader.university

For Soeun

Disclaimer

Neither Little Cash Machines LLC, nor any of its directors, officers, shareholders, personnel, representatives, agents, or independent contractors (collectively, the "Operator Parties") are licensed financial advisers, registered investment advisers, or registered broker-dealers. None of the Operator Parties are providing investment, financial, legal, or tax advice, and nothing in this book or at www.Trader.University (henceforth, "the Site") should be construed as such by you. This book and the Site should be used as educational tools only and are not replacements for professional investment advice. The full disclaimer can be found at the end of this book.

Table of Contents

Your Free Gift

Thanks for purchasing my book!

As a way of showing my appreciation, I want to send you a FREE VIDEO TUTORIAL that contains everything that you need to start using my day trading strategy.

In this free tutorial, you will learn:

- How to set up your chart
- How to screen for good stocks to trade
- Tricks that will make the day trading strategy even more profitable.

Get a copy of this free video tutorial, so that you can start making money today:

http://www.trader.university/day-trading-made-easy-paperback-bonus

Chapter 1: The Magic of Day Trading

In this book, I will teach you a simple but powerful day trading strategy.

I have deliberately made this book very short, so that you can read it quickly and get started making money right away.

But first a word about day trading itself.

In the late 1990's, everyone (and their grandmother) was a successful day trader.

Then the dot-com bubble burst, and day traders lost a lot of money. They stopped bragging about their trading at cocktail parties.

Since then, day trading has become almost a dirty word.

But it turns out that those Nineties traders were not really day traders. They often held positions overnight, or for multiple days.

They ignored risk management. They traded without a stop loss.

The 1995-2000 stock market taught you that if you just held on tight, everything would be OK. Even more, you would be richly rewarded for buying every dip.

That worked for 5 years-- and then suddenly stopped working in early 2000.

Many so-called "day traders" held on to their stocks until they were worth mere pennies. The popular stock CMGI went from 1600 to under 2 in less than 2 years.

Needless to say, that was not a day trade.

So day trading has gotten a bad reputation.

But does that mean that we should now avoid all intraday trades?

When something is out of fashion, it is usually a sign that opportunity is present.

Day trading is, in fact, the fastest way to learn how the markets actually work.

If you love the markets, and are willing to follow them every day, you can learn to day trade profitably.

In the process, you will learn an enormous amount about the markets and about your own personal psychology.

The markets are the best tutor that I know.

And when you've put in your time, you will begin to make money.

On a good day, you will sit down at your trading desk at 9:45 am EST, buy 3,000 shares of a stock, and watch it immediately pop 50 cents.

Ten minutes later, you will sell the stock and pocket $1,500.

It will be 9:55 am on a Monday morning, and you will already have made more money than the average American makes in a week.

Of course, if the trade goes against you, you will have lost more money than the average American makes in a week.

I want you to make money, instead of losing it.

So I am going to teach you a day trading strategy that will help to tilt the odds in your favor.

This strategy is called the "Day Sniper."

It is one of my "bread and butter trades" that I've relied on regularly to pay the bills over the years.

When you are first learning how to day trade, there are many ways to lose, and only one way to win.

Too often, new traders jump from one stock tip to another, from one trading strategy to another, never staying in one place long enough to learn from their mistakes.

The only way to win when you are first starting out is to pick a single trading setup, and then stick with it until you have mastered it.

The Day Sniper is an excellent strategy to begin with.

It is easy to learn, simple to follow, and it will teach you the discipline that is essential to becoming a successful full-time trader.

Once you master the basic strategy, you will learn to alter the strategy to make it fit your own particular style of trading.

The Day Sniper can be used in conjunction with candlestick formations, moving averages, Bollinger Bands, Parabolic SAR, and other indicators that I discuss in my trading courses.

But for now, it is most important to master the basic strategy.

Day trading can be an emotional roller-coaster. More than 90% of day traders lose money over time.

I want you to be part of the 10% that makes money.

And so I am going to give you everything that you need to get started.

First, learn the basic strategy.

Then practice in a paper trading account, or with very small amounts of money.

As you begin to make money, gradually increase the amount of money that you are trading with.

And only then begin to experiment by adding variations to the basic strategy.

Maybe you will delay your initial entry, to try to get a more favorable price.

Maybe you will add to a position on an intraday counter-trend move in order to increase your profits.

Or maybe you will cover your short in the middle of the day, after an especially violent move down, in order to avoid an end-of-day short-covering rally that might eat into your profits.

The more you practice, the more you will be able to bend the rules and trust your gut.

But for now, it's time to learn the basic strategy.

Chapter 2: My Favorite Day Trading Setup

The Day Sniper day trading strategy takes advantage of a basic fact of market structure:

It takes time for big players to enter and exit their positions.

If a mutual fund is holding millions of shares of the stock XYZ, it cannot simply press a button to exit its position.

If XYZ has just reported some very bad news in their latest earnings report, the mutual fund is in a tough spot.

It will take hours, days, or maybe even weeks for the mutual fund to exit its position, depending on the liquidity of the stock.

And the same holds true for a stock that has just reported very good news in its latest earnings report.

If a large mutual fund wants to open a new position (or increase its existing position) in this stock, it will take hours, days, or maybe even weeks for it to do so.

The good news is that smaller traders like you and I can take advantage of these slow, lumbering giants.

Hence, the Day Sniper strategy.

Let's start with an example.

On November 10, 2016, NVIDIA (NVDA) reported much better than expected earnings.

The CEO Jen-Hsun Huang said in the conference call:

"We had a breakout quarter—record revenue, record margins, and record earnings were driven by strength across all product lines."
Right before earnings were released, NVDA had closed at 67.77. After the bullish earnings announcement, the stock immediately traded up about 10% in the after-market trading session.

The next morning, the stock opened up even higher-- at 79.51, up more than 17% from the closing price of the day before.

At this point, even though the stock had already moved up sharply, there were still many institutional investors (mutual funds, hedge funds, and pension funds) who wanted to own more NVDA.

There were many different reasons for this.

Some wanted to be able to show their investors that they owned a lot of a currently fashionable stock.

Some had been short the stock, betting on a bearish earnings report, and now needed to buy shares to cover their shorts.

Some may not have owned any shares, or owned too few shares, and now wanted to increase their positions, because they believed that the company's cash flow or return on assets had fundamentally changed for the better.

Whatever the reason, many institutional investors now needed to buy a lot of NVDA shares.

The problem?

Well, these institutional investors needed to buy millions of shares, which were simply not available all at once.

As a result, they would all need to nibble on the stock, buying a little at a time.

This is where smaller traders like you and I have such a great advantage.

We can run ahead of these slow, lumbering giants, scoop up some shares for ourselves, and then later sell them back to the institutional investors—at a higher price.

This is how the Day Sniper strategy works:

1. Find a stock that is gapping up on good news (like a bullish earnings report).
2. Wait until 15 minutes after the market's open, and note the stock's price at that time.
3. Put in a limit order to buy the stock at that price.

4. If you are not filled in the next 15 minutes, cancel your order and walk away.
5. If you are filled, hold on to the stock and then take profits one minute before the market closes at the end of the day (profit target).
6. Exit the stock early if it trades below the low price of that first 15 minutes of morning trading (stop loss).

It's that simple.

The strategy takes advantage of a stock's tendency to keep moving in the same direction of its morning gap.

What is a gap?

It is simply when a stock moves up or down sharply, leaving a "gap" in the chart that separates it from its previous trading range.

This is what a gap looks like:

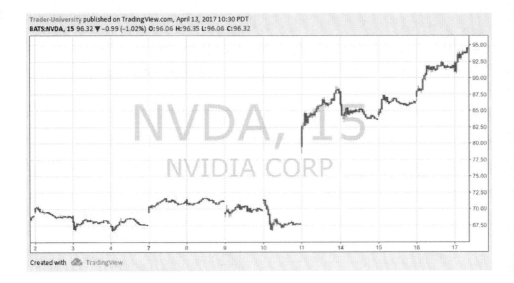

You can see from this chart that NVDA had never traded above 72.50 before.

All of a sudden after the bullish earnings report, it was trading in the high 70's. You can see the striking look of the gap in the chart above.

To trade this strategy, I like to use a chart with 15-minute candlesticks.

You can set up a chart like this using a free service like www.freestockcharts.com.

If you need help setting up your chart, check out my "Free Trading Tutorial" here:

http://www.trader.university/day-trading-made-easy-paperback-bonus

I like to include at least the last 20 days of trading on my 15-minute candlestick chart for the following reason:

You should only take the trade if the stock gaps up above the highest high of the last 20 trading days (or gaps below the lowest low of the last 20 trading days, as we will see in a later chapter on shorting stocks).

A gap that is this dramatic will only occur when there is excessive demand for the stock by buyers.

It will often take the entire day for this excessive demand to be met. This will cause the stock to continue to drift higher, as institutional investors continue to buy the stock.

Let's return to our 15-minute candlestick chart.

You will want to enter your limit order to buy the stock at the closing price of that first 15-minute candlestick.

Your stop loss will be the low of that first 15-minute candlestick. If at any point during the day the stock trades below this price, you should sell it immediately.

If you are not stopped out, you should hold on to the stock until the end of the day. Sell the stock about one or two minutes before the market closes.

If you choose to hold the stock overnight, you're no longer a day trader.

You've become a swing trader.

And that's another strategy for another book.

When you are first starting out, learn the discipline of always exiting at the end of the day.

Go completely to cash, whether the trade has made or lost money, and you will sleep better at night.

Now let's return to the details of our NVDA trade.

After reporting good earnings, the stock gaps up the next morning:

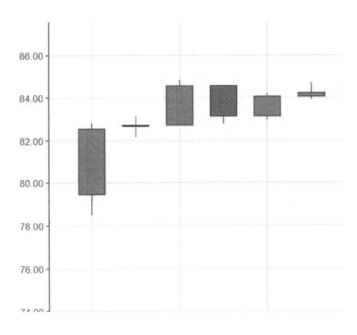

The candlestick on the left shows the first 15 minutes of trading. It opens at 79.51, trades as low as 78.50, as high as 82.82, and then closes at 82.60.

As you can see, when a stock first opens in the morning (6:30 am PST or 9:30 am EST), there is usually a lot of chaos and volatility.

That's why I like to wait until 6:45 am PST (or 9:45 am EST), when the market has been open for 15 minutes, to place my first trade.

So at 6:45 am, we place a limit order to buy NVDA at 82.60 (the closing price of that first 15-minute candlestick).

Within the next 15 minutes, we are filled on our order. We set a mental stop loss at 78.50 (the low of that first 15-minute candlestick). If the stock trades below that price during the day, we are out.

We now hold on to NVDA for the rest of the day, and sell it 1 minute before the market closes at approximately 87.72.

We have captured 5.12 points (87.72-82.60), which comes out to $512 if we've traded 100 shares.

After commissions, that's about $500 net profit for the day.

You would have needed approximately $8,265 in your trading account to buy 100 shares of NVDA at 82.60 (82.60 times 100 plus $5 commission to enter).

There are about 252 trading days in a year, so if we can do this every day, we will be making $126,000 per year.

Even if we can do only half as well (since there will be days when we lose money), we'll still be making $63,000 per year.

To put that in perspective, the median household in the US makes roughly $52,000 per year.

You may wish to trade less aggressively than this when you are first getting started.

So for example, if your targeted entry price is 82.60 and your stop is at 78.50, you will be risking 4.10 points on the trade.

When you are first getting started, it is wise not to risk more than 1% of your trading account on each trade.

So if you are trading a $10,000 account, don't risk more than 1%, which is $100.

If you are risking 4.10 points on this NVDA trade, you should only buy ($100/4.10) or about 24 shares of stock on this trade.

If you buy 24 shares of NVDA at 82.60 and get stopped out at 78.50, you will have lost 4.10 points on 24 shares or about $98 (4.10 times 24).

The closer your entry price is to your stop loss, the more shares you will be able to buy.

For this reason, many traders will only take this trade if they think they can make at least twice the amount that they are risking.

Now let's turn to another example of the Day Sniper strategy at work.

Before the market opened on Tuesday, April 25, 2017, McDonald's (MCD) reported earnings and revenues that beat expectations. All-day breakfast and new sizes for the Big Mac helped to drive up comparable store sales.

So how do we know when a company's earnings report actually beats the expectations?

We can read about the actual EPS reported, and compare it to the analyst consensus projections.

But the only way to be certain that a company has actually beaten the expectations is to witness its stock gapping up in the first 15 minutes of trading like MCD did:

The first 15-minute candlestick of the day closed at 138.87, and had a low of 137.18.

And so fifteen minutes into the trading day, we enter a limit order to buy 100 shares of MCD at 138.87. We are filled on our order immediately.

We then make a mental note that our stop loss is at 137.18 (the low of that first 15-minute candlestick). If MCD trades below that, we will exit our position immediately.

MCD continues to grind higher for most of the day. We exit our position right before the market closes at 141.70.

On this trade, we've captured 2.83 points (141.70-138.87), which is $283 (on 100 shares) before commissions.

It shouldn't cost you more than $5 to enter the trade, and $5 to exit the trade if you are using a good online broker like TradeKing or Interactive Brokers. That leaves you with $273 in profits for the day, after commissions.

Although I haven't used it myself, I've also heard good things about the Robinhood app which allows you to trade for free—no commissions!

In this chapter, we have applied the Day Sniper strategy to stocks that gap up.

In the next chapter, we will discuss how to apply it to stocks that gap down.

Chapter 3: Shorting Stocks Using the Day Sniper Strategy

One of the nice things about the Day Sniper strategy is that it can also be used to trade stocks that are gapping down.

This works especially well in a bear market, when all stocks have a tendency to trade down.

If you learn to trade from both the long and short sides, it will ensure that you will be able to make money in both bull and bear markets.

Let's look at an example of how to short a stock using the strategy.

On March 21, 2017 Nike (NKE) closed at 58.01. It then reported lower than expected quarterly revenue numbers in its earnings report.

The next morning, the stock gapped down 5.60%, opening at 54.76:

In this case, an investor's pain is our gain. I am going to show you how to profit from the stock continuing to sell off for the rest of the day.

The first 15-minute candlestick opened at 54.76, closed at 54.85, and traded as high as 55.00 and as low as 54.23.

In this case, we will be shorting the stock. We will use the order type "sell short" using a limit order at 54.85.

When we are filled, we will place a mental stop loss at the high of that first 15-minute candlestick at 55.00. If the stock trades above that level during the day, we will exit our position immediately.

To exit a short position, we will want to use the order type "buy to cover."

If we are not stopped out, we will wait to exit the position until about 1 minute before the market closes.

In this case, we shorted NKE at 54.85 and covered our short at 53.93 just before the market closed. Trading 100 shares, we captured 0.92 points, or about $92.00 before commissions.

Many new traders are confused about what it means to short a stock.

It's actually quite simple.

When we are buying a stock, we want to buy low and sell high. That's how the money is made.

When we are shorting a stock, we simply reverse the steps:

We first sell high, and then try to buy low.

So how do we sell something that we don't already own?

To short a stock, it is first necessary for the stock to be available to borrow from your broker.

If you have opened up a "margin account" with your broker, you will be able to short sell stocks in your account.

The process of borrowing the shares is usually seamless. There is often a list that you can check to see if the shares are available for shorting.

If it is a well-known name, it should not be a problem to get the shares.

If it is a lesser known name, it may be more difficult.

Be sure to check if there are special fees associated with borrowing a stock to short (such as stock loan fees). Call your brokerage to find out.

Let's look at another example of short selling.

Early on April 18, 2017, Goldman Sachs reported a rare earnings miss. In fact, both earnings and revenues came in below expectations.

The previous day, the stock had closed at 226.26. After reporting earnings before the market opened on April 18, the stock gapped down over 3%, opening up at 219.32.

That open was its lowest trading level for more than the past 20 days:

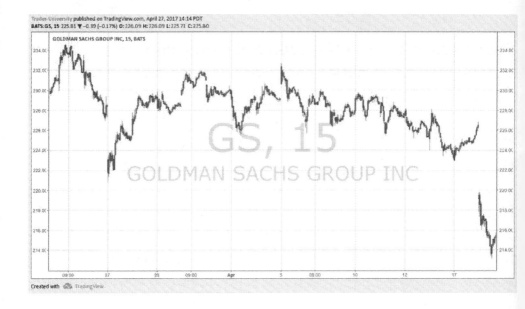

The stock continued to drift lower for much of the rest of the day:

The opening 15-minute candlestick closed at 219.33 and had a high of 219.89.

This proved to be the perfect short trade, since the stop loss (219.89) was so close to the desired entry price (219.33).

So at 6:45 am, we entered an order to sell short 100 shares of GS at 219.33, and were filled.

The next 15-minute bar came close to stopping us out of the trade. It traded as high as 219.85, but fortunately did not breach the 219.89 level where we had (mentally) set our stop loss.

Before we go on, I should remind you to never actually enter your stop loss order directly into the market. If you do this, you run the risk of someone seeing your stop order and trying to run the market to take out your stop.

Rather, write down your stop loss level on a piece of paper, and keep it next to your computer.

If the stock hits that level, exit your position using a limit order that is placed just a penny or two above where the market is currently trading (if you are buying to cover).

If you're desperate to get out, you can also enter a market order, but that is more risky. A market order will get you out, but sometimes at a price that is much further away from the current stock price than you would like.

To get back to our GS trade: we got short at 219.33, and fortunately did not get stopped out when the stock traded as high as 219.85.

The stock continued to move lower until it hit an all-day low of 213.18 at 10:05 am PST.

I have found that around 10 am PST (1 pm EST) can be a great time to take profits, on both the long and short side. You will often end up exiting your trade at the low (or high) of the day.

I am not sure why this anomaly exists, but it may have something to do with traders taking a break for lunch around 12 pm to 1 pm EST. When there is lower liquidity, it is easier for the market to trade more irrationally.

That being said, if you held on to the GS trade until just before the market closed, you still ended up doing very well. You were able to cover your short at 215.59, capturing 3.74 points, or about $374 on 100 shares before commissions.

If you exited at 10 am, you made more like 5.50 points, or $550.

In the next chapter, I will show you the best places to find stocks to day trade using the Day Sniper strategy.

Chapter 4: How to Find the Best Stocks to Day Trade

For the Day Sniper strategy, we are looking for stocks that have just reported earnings, or some other significant news.

My favorite place to find possible candidates for the strategy is the "Trending" list at the top of StockTwits.com (you will need to open a free account with them to view it):

Next to the word "Trending," you can see a list of tickers. If you look here after 1 or 2 pm PST, you are sure to find some stocks that have just reported earnings (assuming that it is earnings season), or that are on the move due to significant news.

You can click on each ticker to see how much the stock is trading up or down. If it is trading more than 3% up or down, search for the ticker on Google News to see what news is moving the stock. You may also see the news in the StockTwits stream itself.

Perhaps it is an earning beat or miss, or perhaps something significant has happened at the company, like the CEO or CFO leaving.

Or perhaps they have "pre-announced" that earnings will come in higher or lower than previously expected.

You can use this to start making a list of stocks that you will want to watch the next morning during the first 15 minutes of trading.

You may be tempted to buy some of these stocks in the after-market hours of trading.

When you are just starting out, you should resist this temptation.

Often a stock will trade significantly higher in the after-hours market after reporting earnings, and then crash 30 minutes later during the earnings call if negative forward guidance is being given.

The after-hours market is extremely volatile, and anything can happen.

Sometimes there may be little or no liquidity (i.e. it will be next to impossible to buy or sell the stock at the price that you are seeing).

It is much better to wait until the following morning, and to watch how the stock trades during that first 15-minute candlestick.

When you are more advanced, and have the courage of your convictions, you may choose to trade in the after-market or pre-market—especially if you follow the company closely, have listened to the earnings call, and are extremely familiar with the company's financial statements, as well as with the industry as a whole.

Until then, stick to the basic Day Sniper strategy.

Another great place to find potential candidates for this strategy is to look at this screener when the market first opens in the morning:

http://www.finviz.com/screener.ashx?v=111&f=ta_perf_d5u&ft=3&o=-price

This screener will provide you with a list of stocks that are trading up more than 5% on the day. You can also change the settings to include stocks that are moving up 10% or more, or down 5% or more.

Once you find a stock that looks interesting, it is important to check the chart to make sure that it is gapping above the last 20-day high, or below the last 20-day low.

At the same time, you can watch the first 15-minute candlestick form, and get ready to place your order at 6:45 am PST if the stock meets all of the necessary criteria.

You can also find good candidates by keeping track of the earnings calendar of stocks. Here are some great places to check:

http://finance.yahoo.com/calendar/earnings

http://www.morningstar.com/earnings/earnings-calendar.aspx

http://www.nasdaq.com/earnings/earnings-calendar.aspx

http://www.marketwatch.com/news/markets/earningswatch.asp

This site will even send you an email alert when a particular ticker reports significant news or earnings:

https://seekingalpha.com/earnings/earnings-calendar

And this site is especially good for finding earnings surprises among well-known names:

http://www.cnbc.com/earnings-surprises/

Most companies will report earnings after the market closes. If you go over these websites every evening, you can create a short list of stocks that you will want to be watching when the market opens the next day.

Some stocks will report earnings in the morning before the stock market opens. These names will also show up in the earnings calendar, and on StockTwits if there is significant movement and interest in the stock.

Chapter 5: How to Avoid the Pattern Day Trader Rule

If you are a trader in the U.S., and you make 4 or more round-trip day trades within a 5-day period in a margin account, you will end up being labeled by the authorities as a "pattern day trader."

A pattern day trader is required by law to maintain a balance of at least $25,000 in his account at all times.

New traders are often discouraged by this rule, which seems to set up a classic catch-22: how can I ever get to $25,000 in my trading account, if you won't let me day trade with a lesser amount?

Fortunately, there are a few ways around this rule.

Before I tell you these ways, I should emphasize that I am not providing legal advice, or advising you in any way what you should actually do with your own trading account. That is a matter between you, your broker, and your financial advisor, of course.

But what I can do here is to tell you what has worked for people that I know.

I know of 5 methods that may be used to bypass the pattern day trader rule.

Method #1

Do your day trading in a "cash account," rather than a "margin account."

In this scenario, you will unfortunately have to wait 3 days after you exit a trade for the cash to be back in your account in order to do another trade. You will also not be able to employ any margin (leverage) in your account. For these reasons, this is probably not the best method.

Method #2

Do only 3 day trades within a rolling 5 business day period.

So if for example you did one day trade on Monday, one on Tuesday, and one on Wednesday, you should not do another day trade until the following Monday (i.e. 3 day trades over 5 trading days).

You can still make a lot of money this way, and start to build up your account. I like this method the most because you can still use leverage (up to 2x in a margin account), but you are forced to trade less frequently and to be more discriminating, taking only the best trades.

Be very careful: if you do a 4th trade within this same rolling 5-day period, your account will be flagged as a pattern day trader account. You will then receive a margin call from your broker that requires you to bring your account balance up to $25,000 within 5 business days.

If you fail to meet this margin call, different things could happen depending on your broker. In most cases, your buying power will be restricted for 90 days, or until the margin call is met (the account balance is brought up to $25,000).

You should call your own broker to find out exactly how they handle the pattern day trader rule.

You can read about how TradeKing handles the pattern day trader rule here:

http://www.tradeking.com/investing/day-trading-rules

Method #3

Hold your trades overnight, especially if you have already done 3 day trades in the last rolling 5-day period.

If you hold a trade overnight, it will not count towards the 4 trades, since an overnight trade is not a day trade.

Unfortunately, holding a stock overnight will definitely expose you to more risk. You may make more money as a result, but you can also lose money.

Literally anything can happen overnight in the worlds of geopolitics or business.

On the other hand, if you are using a trailing stop in your trade, and you have still not been stopped out by the end of the day, you may wish to hold overnight.

Or if the stock is finishing at the highs (or lows, if you are short the stock) of the day, you may also wish to hold the position overnight. These strong moves will often continue overnight and into the opening minutes of the next trading day.

Method #4

Split your cash between two separate brokerage accounts.

So if you have $10,000, you could open up an account at TradeKing with $5,000 and an account at Interactive Brokers with $5,000.

Using this method, you can do 6 day trades in a rolling 5 business day period (3 trades in each account as in method #3).

Method #5

This final method will allow you to do an unlimited number of day trades.

First, split your trading account across 2 brokerages as in method #5. Put $5,000 at TradeKing or wherever, and $5,000 at Interactive Brokers, or wherever.

But in this case, you will do something especially sneaky. Let's say that today you bought 100 shares of NVDA in your TradeKing account. At the end of the day, instead of selling the shares, simply sell short 100 shares of NVDA in your Interactive Brokers account.

This will zero-out your exposure to the stock, in effect taking profits. If NVDA falls overnight, you will lose money in your TradeKing account, but you will make back the same amount of money on your short NVDA position in your Interactive Brokers account.

The following morning, you can exit your long NVDA position and your short NVDA position. Since each one was held overnight, neither trade will count toward your 3 allowed day trades.

This latter method may just be a bit too clever. I'll leave it up to your own judgment.

When you are first starting out, it might be better to stick to making 3 day trades over every rolling 5 trading day period.

Keep following the Day Sniper trading rules that we learned in chapter 2, until you have learned to always stick to your stop loss.

And make sure that you exit your day trade every single time by the end of the trading day.

Remember that only losers hold a losing day trade overnight.

Once you have established this sort of trading discipline, feel free to experiment with different kinds of trailing stops like moving averages, Parabolic SAR, and 3-line break.

If you'd like to learn more about these advanced methods, you can check out my course "Learn to Trade Stocks like a Pro" at http://www.trader.university.

Chapter 6: The Next Step

We've covered a lot of ground in this book. I hope that you are ready to take this information and use it to start making money for yourself trading.

The best way to learn about trading is to just start doing it. Start with very small positions, and then slowly increase them as your capital (and your confidence!) increases.

There's no better way to learn than simply by doing.

And I'm here to help you on your journey to becoming a professional trader.

If you have questions, or just want to say hi, write to me at matt@trader.university

I love to hear from my readers, and I answer every email personally.

Before you go, I'd like to say "thank you" for purchasing this book and reading it all the way to the end.

If you enjoyed this book and found it useful, I'd be very grateful if you'd post an honest review on Amazon. All you need to do is to go to **www.trader-books.com** and click on the correct book cover.

Then click the blue link next to the yellow stars that says "customer reviews." You'll then see a gray button that says "Write a customer review"—click that and you will be able to submit your review to Amazon.

If you would like to learn more ways to make money in the markets, check out my other Kindle books on the next page.

TRADER UNIVERSITY

THE LITTLE BLACK BOOK OF STOCK MARKET SECRETS

MATTHEW R. KRATTER

The Little Black Book of Stock Market Secrets

Rocket Stocks: Learn to Profit from the Stock Market's Biggest Winners

Invest Like Warren Buffett: Powerful Strategies for Building Wealth

Monthly Cash Machine:Powerful Strategies for Selling Options in Bull and Bear Markets

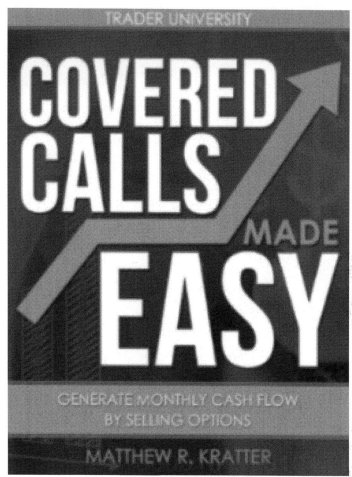

Covered Calls Made Easy
The Amazon #1 Bestseller for Options Trading

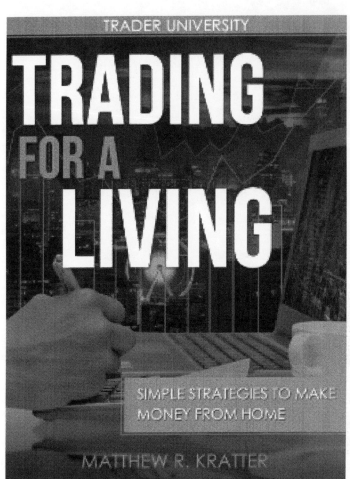

Trading For A Living

Learn to Trade Momentum Stocks

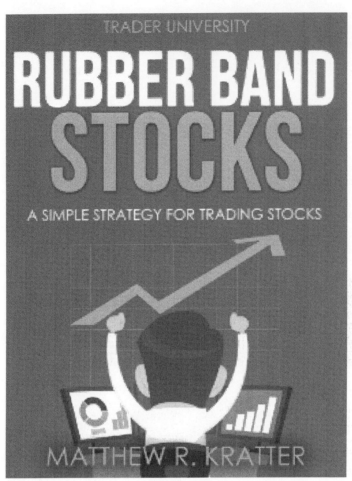

Rubber Band Stocks: A Simple Strategy for Trading Stocks

Your Free Gift

Thanks for purchasing my book!

As a way of showing my appreciation, I want to send you a FREE VIDEO TUTORIAL that contains everything that you need to start using my day trading strategy.

In this free tutorial, you will learn:

- How to set up your chart
- How to screen for good stocks to trade
- Tricks that will make the day trading strategy even more profitable.

Get a copy of this free video tutorial, so that you can start making money today:

http://www.trader.university/day-trading-made-easy-paperback-bonus

About the Author

Hi there!

My name is Matthew Kratter. I am the founder of Trader University, and the best-selling author of multiple books on trading and investing. I have more than 20 years of trading experience, including working at multiple hedge funds.

Most individual traders and investors are at a huge disadvantage when it comes to the markets. Most are unable to invest in hedge funds. Yet, when they trade their own money, they are competing against computer algorithms, math PhD's, and multi-billion dollar hedge funds. I've been on the inside of many hedge funds. I know how professional traders and investors think and approach the markets. And I am committed to sharing their trading strategies with you in my books and courses.

When I am not trading or writing new books, I enjoy bodysurfing and otherwise hanging out at the beach with my wife, kids, and labradoodle.

If you enjoyed this book, you will also enjoy my other Kindle titles, which are available here:

http://www.Trader-Books.com/

Or send me an email at matt@trader.university. I would love to hear from you.

Disclaimer

While the author has used his best efforts in preparing this book, he makes no representations or warranties with respect to the accuracy or completeness of the contents of this book and specifically disclaims any implied warranties or merchantability or fitness for a particular purpose. The advice and strategies contained herein may not be suitable for your situation. You should consult with a legal, financial, tax, or other professional where appropriate. Neither the publisher nor the author shall be liable for any loss of profit or any other commercial damages, including but not limited to special, incidental, consequential, or other damages.

This book is for educational purposes only. The views expressed are those of the author alone, and should not be taken as expert instruction or commands. The reader is responsible for his or her own actions.

Adherence to all applicable laws and regulations, including international, federal, state, and local laws governing professional licensing, business practices, advertising, and all other aspects of doing business in the US, Canada, or any other jurisdiction is the sole responsibility of the purchaser or reader.

Neither the author nor the publisher assumes any responsibility or liability whatsoever on the behalf of the purchaser or reader of these materials.

Any perceived slight of any individual or organization is purely unintentional.

Made in the USA
Monee, IL
29 June 2021